MICROWAVE VEGETABLE DISHES & SNACKS

OTHER NO NONSENSE COOKING GUIDES

Cookies for Holidays & Every Day
Entertaining at Home
Appetizers, Hors d'Oeuvres & Salads
Breakfasts & Brunches
Microwave Diet Cooking
Fabulous Desserts: Mainly Microwave
Microwave Main Courses, Quick & Easy

OTHER NO NONSENSE GUIDES

Real Estate Guides
Financial Guides
Business Guides
Legal Guides
Wine Guides
Home Repair Guides
Health Guides
Success Guides

MICROWAVE VEGETABLE DISHES & SNACKS

IRENA CHALMERS

LONGMEADOW PRESS

MICROWAVE VEGETABLE DISHES & SNACKS

Copyright © 1987 by Irena Chalmers

Published by Longmeadow Press, 201 High Ridge Road, Stamford, Connecticut 06904. No part of this book may be reproduced or used in any form or by any means, electronic or mechanical, including photocopying, recording, or by an information storage and retrieval system, without permission in writing from the publisher.

ISBN 0-681-40271-7

Printed in the United States of America

0 9 8 7 6 5 4 3 2

STAFF FOR NO NONSENSE COOKING GUIDES

EDITORIAL DIRECTION: **Jean Atcheson**

MANAGING EDITOR: **Mary Goodbody**

COVER DESIGN: **Karen Skelton**

ART DIRECTION & DESIGN: **Helene Berinsky**

RECIPE DEVELOPMENT: **Marilyn Schanze, Cynthia Salvino**
AMERICAN COOKING INSTITUTE, ST. JOSEPH, MICHIGAN

ASSISTANT EDITORS: **Mary Dauman, Dorothy Atcheson**

PROJECT MANAGER: **Nancy Kipper**

COVER PHOTOGRAPH: **Gerald Zanetti**

TYPESETTING: **ComCom, Allentown, Pennsylvania**

PRODUCTION SERVICES: **William S. Konecky Associates, New York**

CONTENTS

ACKNOWLEDGMENTS

Grateful acknowledgment is made to the following for permission to reproduce or adapt original recipes:

Bounty Microwave Paper Towels, Procter and Gamble; Campbell Soup Company; Corning Glass Works; Hellmann's and Best Foods, CPC International, Inc.; Ms. Thelma Pressman; The Quaker Oats Company; Reynolds Metal Company

MICROWAVE VEGETABLE DISHES AND SNACKS

V egetables are the food of our times. A generation or two ago they were generally plunked in boiling water and then spooned onto a plate simply to round out a meal of meat and potatoes. No longer! These days, they have taken on a starring role, upstaging red meat and heavy creamy sauces with their lightness, freshness, brilliant color and all-around goodness.

More and more cooks are buying their vegetables fresh, though there is still a welcome place for them in frozen and canned forms. With the proliferation of greengrocers, expanded produce departments in supermarkets and specialty stores, and the steadily increasing interest in home gardening, fresh vegetables can be found in kitchens all across America. Thanks to improved cultivation and shipping, familiar and exotic vegetables are available to the home cook nearly all year long. Not only have we become accustomed to Bibb, Boston and radicchio lettuce (once thought very esoteric greens indeed), but we readily purchase items such as bok choy (Chinese cabbage), endive, "wild" mushrooms, leeks, scallions, yellow and black bell peppers, and white eggplant.

After an excursion to the market, our shopping baskets bulge with a colorful jumble of vegetables. They look so tempting, who can resist them? Luckily, when we arrive home, the microwave makes the cooking of this array of bounty fast, simple and efficient.

First and foremost, vegetables taste good, but no one denies that they are very good for us, too. Boiling them to mushy pulp not only destroys their flavor but depletes vegetables of most of their valuable nutrients. Cooking them in the microwave retains their distinctive flavors, high color and wonderful textures *and* most of the vitamins and minerals as well.

Microwaves agitate water molecules, causing the friction necessary to heat and eventually cook food. Vegetables, with their high water content, cook particularly well in the microwave oven. Whole fresh artichokes, wrapped in transparent wrap to hold in moisture, are ready in less than 10 minutes. A cup or two of sliced carrots with a mere tablespoon or so of water cooks in five or six minutes; a whole acorn squash is done in about 10 or 11 minutes. Baking potatoes emerge from the microwave in less than 10 minutes fully cooked, fluffy and steaming. It is even possible to put a rock-hard package of frozen spinach or string beans or another vegetable (always puncture the package first to allow steam to escape) in the microwave and after seven or eight minutes, eat perfectly cooked food.

Vegetables cooked to crisp-tender goodness in the microwave are so delicious on their own that often you will desire no more embellishment than a squeeze of lemon juice and a little salt and pepper. Other times, you will want to produce full-flavored and rich vegetable casseroles, soups and medleys to serve as eye-catching side dishes or warm and filling main courses. In either event, the microwave is invaluable, as are the recipes in this book.

Follow the instructions for covering, venting and standing times carefully. Be a little more flexible when it comes to cooking times. As with nearly all cooking, the degree of doneness depends largely on personal taste. You may prefer your vegetables softer than some people, or you may like them crunchy. Never hesitate to open the door of the microwave (it will stop emitting waves as soon as the door opens) to check the food. Adjust the cooking times to suit your own needs as well as the size and shape of the food.

These guidelines hold true in all areas of microwave cooking, and especially when you turn to the chapters on savory and sweet snacks. Here are recipes for granola mixes, muffins, quick breads, vegetable dips, sandwiches and popcorn. Many of the recipes can also be used for more substantial meals (the muffins are great for breakfast), but all will fill that gap between meals when we need *something* to tide us over—and preferably something tasty, quick and relatively healthy. Once again, the microwave comes in handy, aiding the fast preparation of food that tastes just as good as it looks.

USING YOUR MICROWAVE

MICROWAVE POWER AND TIMING

Most microwaves run on 600 to 700 watts, although some of the smaller models are less powerful. The recipes in this book have been developed for microwaves within this range but if yours is less than 600 watts, you will need to extend slightly the cooking times given in recipes.

Microwave cooking is not an exact science, so you cannot depend on time alone to determine when the food is cooked. Open the oven door during cooking to check the food for doneness and adjust times and power settings accordingly, just as you would in a conventional oven.

Remember: The amount of power can also be affected by various factors, such as use of other electrical equipment on the same circuit or even utility company procedures.

The temperature, size and shape of the food will affect the timing, too. Food at room temperature cooks more quickly than food just taken from the refrigerator.

POWER SETTINGS

Most of today's microwave ovens offer variable power settings ranging from High (100 percent power) to Low (10 percent). The higher settings are most often used for cooking or reheating, while the low settings are designed for simmering, defrosting or keeping food warm. Throughout this book, we have indicated the power percentage necessary for every recipe.

EQUIPMENT

You do not need any special utensils for basic microwave cooking, although as you become more adventurous you may want to invest in some of the equipment specially designed for the microwave, such as browning dishes or racks.

You cannot use metal containers, most aluminum foil, or even plates with a metallic trim because microwaves cannot pass through metal. If you put metal in the microwave, the waves will bounce off the metal and "arc," which means they will spark and sizzle. In some modern ovens, however, lightweight aluminum foil may be used for shielding parts of the food that might otherwise overcook.

Heatproof glass plates and dishes are ideal, as are most ceramics, porcelain or pottery. Test any utensil you are unsure about before using it in the microwave.

TESTING FOR "MICROWAVABILITY"

Put the utensil in the oven along with a 1-cup glass measure filled with tap water. Microwave on High (100 percent power) for 1 minute. If the dish remains cool while the water in the measure becomes hot, the utensil is safe to use, or "microwavable." If the dish becomes hot, it is absorbing microwave energy and should not be used. (During cooking, the transfer of heat from food *can* make microwavable dishes hot, so be sure to have potholders handy.)

MICROWAVE COOKING TECHNIQUES

Small, uniformly shaped pieces or amounts of food will cook more quickly than large. Shield the thinner parts of unevenly shaped foods to prevent overcooking.

Stir or rearrange food once or twice during the cooking process to help it cook more evenly. Rotating foods in the oven will achieve the same result.

Remember: Standing time is often part of cooking. Some foods will not seem completely cooked when removed from the microwave but the standing time will complete the process.

Use paper towels and plates, transparent wrap and wax paper in the microwave according to the recipe instructions. Dry plain white paper towels prevent spattering and absorb moisture. Wax paper makes a loose cover to hold in heat.

When a tight cover is needed to hold in steam and tenderize and cook food more evenly, use a casserole lid or transparent wrap rolled back slightly at one edge to allow for venting. Be careful of escaping steam as you remove a cover.

CHAPTER 1

GREEN VEGETABLES

Because green vegetables round out a meal so nicely, because they provide so many nutrients and because they taste so good, we are constantly looking for new and better ways to prepare them. The microwave makes it easy. Fresh and frozen vegetables cook quickly and evenly, few vitamins and minerals escape during cooking, and the flavors are honest and colors vibrant.

Green vegetables such as green beans, asparagus, artichokes, broccoli, snow peas and cauliflower (which is not actually green but belongs in this category nonetheless) blend deliciously with a grand array of herbs, cheeses and seasonings. Concocting recipes with these ingredients is more successful in the microwave than by conventional methods, and far faster. And as many of the recipes require only one dish or a simple covering of paper towels or transparent wrap, cleaning up is a breeze.

Oriental Vegetables

Serves 4

Steamed vegetables retain their color, texture and flavor. In this recipe, crisp pea pods and bok choy are enclosed in a paper towel packet which is moistened with broth or water. To make the packet, first fold the long sides of the paper towels toward the center and then bring up the shorter ends so that the food is completely enclosed. Bok choy is sometimes called Chinese cabbage. Enoki mushrooms, boxed in plastic, can be found in many supermarkets and Asian groceries.

> *2 tablespoons vegetable oil*
> *1 teaspoon sesame oil*
> *¼ teaspoon crushed dried red pepper*
> *½ pound fresh snow pea pods, trimmed*
> *2 cups thinly sliced bok choy*
> *½ cup chicken broth or water*
> *1 cup enoki mushrooms (optional)*
> *Soy sauce*

Combine the vegetable oil, sesame oil and red pepper in a microwavable casserole. Microwave on High (100 percent) for 1 to 2 minutes, until hot.

Add the snow pea pods and bok choy and toss to combine. Lay 2 connected paper towels on the counter and put half the vegetables on top, over the perforations. Fold the towels to enclose the vegetables. Repeat with the remaining vegetables and set both packets on a large microwavable plate. Pour half the chicken broth over each packet and microwave on High (100 percent) for 7 to 10 minutes, until the vegetables are crisp-tender. Rotate the plate once during the cooking time.

Remove the vegetables from the oven and let stand for 2 minutes. Open the packet along the perforations. Stir in the mushrooms, if you are using them, sprinkle with soy sauce and serve.

Use only unprinted white paper towels in the microwave—preferably those specifically designed and labeled for microwave use.

Italian-Style Green Beans

Serves 4

Scallions and tomatoes blend nicely with green beans for a fresh, new look. The juice from the tomatoes, thickened with a little cornstarch, makes a tasty sauce.

Frozen vegetables can be completely cooked in the microwave without ever leaving their packages. Strip off the paper wrapping, punch a few holes in the top of the cardboard box and microwave on High (100 percent) for 4 to 7 minutes, until done.

2 tablespoons chopped scallions
1 tablespoon (½ ounce) butter
2 cups frozen cut green beans
1 cup chopped tomatoes, juice reserved
½ teaspoon finely chopped garlic
¼ teaspoon dried thyme
⅛ teaspoon pepper
1½ teaspoons cornstarch
1 tablespoon cold water

Combine the scallions and butter in a 1-quart microwavable casserole. Microwave on High (100 percent) for 2 to 3 minutes.

Stir in the green beans, chopped tomatoes, reserved juices, garlic, thyme and pepper. Cover and microwave on High (100 percent) for 6 to 9 minutes, stirring after 3½ minutes, until the beans are crisp-tender.

Dissolve the cornstarch in 1 tablespoon of cold water and stir it into the vegetables. Cover and microwave on High (100 percent) for 1 to 2 minutes until thickened and bubbly. Allow the vegetables to stand for 2 minutes before serving.

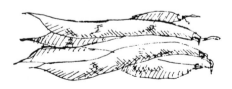

Vegetable Medley Pasta

Serves 4

Offer this colorful pasta either as a main course or a side dish. Green pasta is egg pasta with spinach worked into the dough; adding carrot or tomato makes pasta red. If you cannot find colored pastas, make it with plain egg pasta—it will be just as tasty.

> 2 cups broccoli florets
> ½ cup green pepper strips, each ¼ by 2 inches
> ½ cup pepper strips, each ¼ by 2 inches
> ¼ cup vegetable oil
> 3 tablespoons red wine vinegar
> ½ teaspoon sugar
> ¼ teaspoon salt
> ¼ teaspoon dried oregano
> ¼ teaspoon dried basil
> ⅛ teaspoon dry mustard
> ⅛ teaspoon cayenne pepper
> 1 clove garlic, finely chopped
> 2 cups hot egg, spinach and carrot or tomato pasta, cooked and drained
> ½ cup pitted black olives

Put the broccoli and the green and red pepper strips in a 2½-quart microwavable casserole. Microwave on High (100 percent) for 1½ to 2 minutes, stirring after 1 minute.

Combine the oil, vinegar, sugar, salt, oregano, basil, mustard, cayenne pepper and garlic in a 1-cup glass measure. Microwave on High (100 percent) for 1½ minutes, stirring after 1 minute.

Toss the hot pasta with the vegetables and the olives. Pour the hot dressing over the pasta mixture and toss to coat. Serve immediately.

Stuffed Artichokes

Serves 4

Give artichokes extra pizzazz with a spinach stuffing flavored with scallions and garlic, and add a topping of melted cheese.

4 medium-size artichokes
¼ cup lemon juice
¼ cup water
¼ cup chopped scallions
¼ cup chopped celery
1 clove garlic, finely chopped
1 tablespoon (½ ounce) butter
12-ounce package frozen spinach soufflé, thawed
½ cup fine dry bread crumbs
1 tablespoon chopped parsley
Dash pepper
½ cup grated cheddar cheese

Never hesitate to open the microwave oven door during cooking time to test food for doneness—especially important when cooking vegetables that should be crisp-tender and not overcooked.

Trim the artichoke stems close to the base and brush the leaves with lemon juice. Fit a microwavable 2½-quart roasting pan with a rack, set the artichokes on the rack and add the water. Cover the pan with heavy-duty transparent wrap and microwave on High (100 percent) for 6 to 7 minutes, or until the artichokes are just tender, rotating the pan a half turn halfway through the cooking time. Set the artichokes aside.

Put the scallions, celery, garlic and butter in a microwavable 1-quart casserole and microwave on High (100 percent) for 2 to 3 minutes, or until the vegetables are tender, stirring halfway through the cooking time.

Add the thawed spinach, bread crumbs, parsley and pepper to the casserole and stir the vegetables. Spread the center leaves of each artichoke to form a well. If you like, you can remove some of the center leaves and scrape out the choke, to make room for more stuffing. Stuff the artichokes with the spinach mixture.

Arrange the artichokes again in the roasting pan and cover with heavy-duty transparent wrap. Microwave on High (100 percent) for 6 to 7 minutes, until the stuffing is hot, the base of each artichoke is tender and the leaves can be removed with a slight tug. Rotate the pan a half turn during the cooking time.

Sprinkle the cheese evenly over the artichokes and re-cover the pan with transparent wrap. Microwave on High (100 percent) for 1 to 2 minutes, until the cheese melts. Rotate the pan a half turn during the cooking time. Serve at once.

Almond Asparagus

Serves 4

Almonds and water chestnuts provide the texture here, while soy sauce adds an unmistakably Asian flair.

> *2 tablespoons (1 ounce) butter*
> *2 tablespoons sliced almonds*
> *10-ounce package frozen cut asparagus*
> *½ cup diagonally sliced celery*
> *8-ounce can sliced water chestnuts*
> *1 tablespoon soy sauce*

Combine the butter and the almonds in a 1½-quart microwavable casserole. Microwave on High (100 percent) for 3 to 4 minutes until the nuts are golden brown, stirring occasionally. Remove the almonds from the casserole.

Put the asparagus, celery, and water chestnuts in the casserole. Cover and microwave on High (100 percent) for 5 to 6 minutes, stirring halfway through cooking time.

Stir in the soy sauce and almonds. Cover the casserole and let it stand for 2 minutes before serving.

Broccoli Stir-Fry

Serves 4

Using a browning skillet gives this vegetable mixture the flavor and texture of a stir-fry, but if you have no browning skillet, the dish will still taste good. Be sure to test the vegetables partway through cooking to judge the correct total cooking time.

> *1 tablespoon vegetable oil*
> *1 clove garlic, finely chopped*
> *2 cups broccoli florets, fresh or frozen*
> *¼ cup sliced red pepper*
> *¼ cup sliced mushrooms*
> *2 teaspoons soy sauce*

Put the oil and garlic in a glass measure. Microwave on High (100 percent) for 1 minute, until the garlic softens and the oil is hot.

If you are using frozen broccoli florets, puncture the package and microwave on High (100 percent) for 2 to 3 minutes. Separate the florets and put them in an 8- or 10-inch microwave browning skillet. Add the peppers and mushrooms and stir to mix.

Pour the oil and garlic over the vegetables. Sprinkle with the soy sauce.Cover and microwave on High (100 percent) for 4 to 7 minutes, until the broccoli and peppers are crisp-tender. Stir after 3 minutes and test to adjust the cooking time.

Pea Pods and Wild Rice

Serves 6 to 8

Pea pods and pimientos contribute color while the wild rice and optional cashews add crunchiness.

> 1 tablespoon cornstarch
> 6¼-ounce box long grain and wild rice
> 1¾ cups water
> 6 ounces snow pea pods, trimmed and cut into pieces
> ½ cup chopped celery
> 2-ounce jar pimientos, drained and chopped
> 2 tablespoons (1 ounce) butter, cut into pieces
> ½ cup chopped cashews (optional)

Shake the cornstarch in a 14-by-20-inch microwavable cooking bag. Add the remaining ingredients, except the cashews to the cooking bag and seal securely. Turn the bag to distribute the ingredients. Make 6 ½-inch slits in the top of the bag and put it in a 12-by-8-by-2-inch microwavable baking dish.

Microwave on High (100 percent) for 8 to 10 minutes, until the rice is tender. Rotate the pan one half turn during the cooking time and manipulate the bag to mix the ingredients. Sprinkle the cashews on top, if you are using them, and serve.

BAGGING IT

When a recipe calls for a microwave cooking bag, it means a plastic bag sold with nylon or plastic ties. Very often, what you think of as a plastic storage bag is labeled as being microwavable as well. These bags are handy—you can fill them with food and store them in the refrigerator. However, they must be vented before they are placed in the microwave to allow steam to escape and reduce the risk of a bag exploding.

CHAPTER 2

TOMATOES, MUSHROOMS AND EGGPLANT

Tomatoes and eggplant are among the stars of any summer vegetable garden. During the months of August and September, it is hard to think of eating tomatoes any way except raw with perhaps a sprinkling of salt, a grinding of pepper or a drizzle of olive oil. But summer tomatoes—and those available at other times of year—can be cooked into so many tantalizing dishes that it is a shame not to try them. Eggplant, too, is an amazingly versatile vegetable with a flavor that blends well with other vegetables, herbs and cheese. Add mushrooms to the grouping, and you have three winners when it comes to making vegetable casseroles and medleys.

All three are full of moisture and cook quickly and evenly in the microwave. They rarely require much more tending than a stir partway through cooking and minimal, if any, standing time. And their rich flavors and soft, pleasing textures come through every time.

Italian Eggplant and Mushrooms

Serves 2 to 4

Combining tender young purple and white eggplants looks picturesque, but if white eggplant is hard to find, the dish will taste good made with the purple ones.

> *¾ pound (about 8) baby purple and white*
> *eggplants*
> *2 teaspoons salt*
> *1 clove garlic, finely chopped*
> *1 tablespoon chopped fresh basil*
> *1 cup sliced fresh mushrooms*
> *¼ medium-size green pepper, cut into thin strips*
> *⅓ cup water*
> *1 tablespoon olive oil*

Trim the eggplants and cut them lengthwise into ¼-inch slices. Arrange the slices in a single layer on a large plate. Sprinkle them with the salt and let stand for 10 minutes. Rinse well and drain in a large colander.

Lay a sheet of paper towel on a microwavable plate. Put the eggplant slices in the center of the paper towel and top with the garlic, basil, mushrooms and green pepper.

Fold the corners of the paper towel over the vegetables. Top with another sheet and tuck the corners under the packet. Pour the water evenly over the packet and microwave on High (100 percent) for 6½ to 9 minutes, until the vegetables are tender, rotating the plate once during cooking.

Remove the packet from the microwave and let stand for 2 minutes. Open the packet, arrange the vegetables in a bowl and sprinkle them with the olive oil just before serving.

Salting eggplant before cooking leaches excess moisture from the vegetable. Be sure to rinse and drain it well.

Corn and Tomato Casserole

Serves 6

For the true flavor of summer, make this dish with sun-ripened tomatoes and locally grown corn.

> *4 medium-size tomatoes*
> *3 tablespoons (1½ ounces) butter*
> *1 onion, finely chopped*
> *2 stalks celery, finely chopped*
> *1 green pepper, stemmed, seeded and finely chopped*
> *3 tablespoons all-purpose flour*
> *1½ cups milk*
> *Salt and pepper*
> *3 large egg yolks*
> *½ cup grated parmesan cheese*
> *3 large hard-cooked eggs, peeled and sliced*
> *2 cups fresh corn kernels*
> *Parsley, for garnish*

Peeling tomatoes is easy with the microwave. Put enough water in a bowl to cover the tomatoes and microwave (before adding the tomatoes) until boiling. Carefully drop the tomatoes into the water for a few seconds and you will find their skins peel off easily. This technique works with peaches, too.

Peel, seed and chop 3 of the tomatoes. Slice the remaining tomato.

Put the butter in a microwavable casserole and microwave on High (100 percent) for 1 minute. Add the onion, celery and green pepper and microwave on High (100 percent) for 2 minutes, stirring after 1 minute, until the onion is softened.

Stir in the flour and microwave on High (100 percent) for 30 seconds. Stir in the milk with a wire whisk and season with salt and pepper. Microwave on High (100 percent) for 2 to 4 minutes, until the sauce has thickened. Add the egg yolks and the parmesan cheese and stir to blend.

Arrange the chopped tomatoes, sliced eggs and corn in a 10-inch microwavable baking dish and pour the sauce over the top. Cover with wax paper and micro-wave on Low (30 percent) for 7 to 9 minutes, stirring after the first 2 minutes. Let stand for 2 minutes. Top with the tomato slices and garnish with parsley.

Mushroom Sauté

Serves 8

Mushrooms and green peppers served in a sweet-sour sauce—unusual? Perhaps. Delicious? Absolutely.

> ¼ cup packed brown sugar
> 1½ teaspoons cornstarch
> ⅛ teaspoon pepper
> 2 tablespoons Dijon mustard
> 2 tablespoons Worcestershire sauce
> ⅓ cup red wine
> 1 onion, cut into eighths
> 1 pound fresh mushrooms, cleaned and cut in half
> 1¼ cups 1-inch pieces of green pepper

Always wipe mushrooms clean with a damp cloth. If they are rinsed under running water or soaked, they absorb unnecessary liquid.

Combine the brown sugar, cornstarch, pepper, mustard, Worcestershire sauce, and wine in a 2-cup glass measure. Microwave on High (100 percent) for 1 minute. Add the onion pieces. Microwave on High (100 percent) for 2 to 3 minutes, until the onion softens. Stir after 1 minute.

Put the mushrooms and green pepper in a 2½-quart microwavable casserole.

Add the sauce and onion. Cover and microwave on High (100 percent) for 5 to 7 minutes, stirring twice, until the vegetables are tender but not soft.

Spanish Eggs

Serves 4

This simple brunch or supper dish is a good way of using up leftovers.

1 tablespoon vegetable oil
¼ small onion, finely chopped
1 clove garlic, finely chopped
½ green pepper, stemmed, seeded and finely chopped
½ cup cooked pork or chicken, diced
½ cup cooked ham, diced
2 tablespoons all-purpose flour
¾ cup chicken broth
1½ teaspoons chopped fresh basil or ½ teaspoon dried
1 tomato, peeled, seeded and chopped
Salt and pepper
2 tablespoons (1 ounce) butter
4 large eggs
Parsley, for garnish

Puncturing the yolks of the eggs before microwaving them insures that they will not burst.

Eggs should be slightly undercooked when microwaved and then allowed to stand, covered, to complete the cooking process.

Combine the oil, onion, garlic and green pepper in an 8-inch glass pie plate. Microwave on High (100 percent) for 1 minute until the onion is softened.

Add the pork and ham. Stir in the flour and add the chicken broth and basil. Microwave on High (100 percent) for 3 minutes. Add the tomato and microwave on High (100 percent) for 1 minute. Season to taste with salt and pepper and set aside.

Put the butter in a shallow microwavable dish and microwave on High (100 percent) for 1 minute or until melted. Break the eggs onto the dish and pierce the yolks with a fork. Microwave on Medium (50 percent) for 3 to 5 minutes or until set. Slide the eggs onto the meat and vegetables and garnish with parsley.

Ratatouille

Serves 8

Whether you serve it hot or cold, ratatouille, chock-full of tomatoes and eggplant, is a long-standing favorite.

3 tablespoons olive oil
1 medium-size onion, finely chopped
3 cloves garlic, finely chopped
1 medium-size eggplant, quartered lengthwise and cut into ⅛-inch slices
2 medium-size zucchini, cut into ⅛-inch slices
3–4 cups chopped tomatoes with any juice
3 tablespoons tomato paste
1 tablespoon chopped fresh basil or 1½ teaspoons dried
½ teaspoon dried thyme
1 teaspoon salt
⅛ teaspoon pepper

Combine the olive oil, onion and garlic in a 3½-quart microwavable casserole. Cover and microwave on High (100 percent) for 2 to 3 minutes, stirring after 1½ minutes, until the onion is softened.

Stir in the eggplant and replace the cover. Microwave on High (100 percent) for 2 to 3 minutes, stirring after 1 minute, until the eggplant softens a little.

Add the zucchini, the tomatoes and their juice, the tomato paste, herbs and seasoning. Microwave on High (100 percent) for 10 to 12 minutes, stirring every 4 minutes until the vegetables are tender.

Stuffed Tomatoes

Serves 6

While this is best made with vine-ripened tomatoes and fresh garden basil, it is also a flavorful cold-weather vegetable dish. If you make it in the fall or winter, it is a good idea to let the tomatoes sit at room temperature for a few days to ripen further, even if they *look* ripe when you buy them.

> 6 large firm tomatoes
> 1 cup dry toasted bread crumbs
> 1 tablespoon chopped fresh basil or 1½ teaspoons dried
> ¼ cup chopped parsley
> 2 tablespoons chopped scallions
> 2 cloves garlic, finely chopped
> ½ teaspoon dried thyme
> ½ teaspoon salt
> ⅛ teaspoon pepper
> Lemon wedges, for garnish

Slice the top from each tomato and scoop out the pulp. Drain the pulp and chop it coarsely. Invert and drain the tomato shells on paper towels.

Combine the tomato pulp with the bread crumbs, basil, parsley, scallions, garlic, thyme, salt and pepper. Spoon the stuffing mixture into the tomatoes.

Arrange the stuffed tomatoes in a 12-by-7-by-2-inch microwavable casserole. Microwave on High (100 percent) for 3 minutes. Rotate the dish a half turn and microwave on High (100 percent) for 3 to 5 minutes, until the tomatoes are hot and fork-tender. Serve garnished with lemon wedges.

Tomato Soup

Serves 6

Microwaves are ideal for making soups from scratch because the cooking time is so brief. Tomato soup is at its best in the summer when the tomatoes are full of superb flavor.

> *2 pounds Italian plum tomatoes or about*
> *   6 medium-size tomatoes*
> *1 onion, chopped*
> *1 stalk celery, chopped*
> *2 cups chicken broth*
> *1 tablespoon tomato paste*
> *1 teaspoon dried basil or oregano*
> *1 teaspoon salt*
> *Pepper*
> *1 cup yogurt, sour cream or heavy cream (optional)*

A ripe tomato feels heavy and full and has a clear rosy color that varies from bright to deep red.

Cut the plum tomatoes in half or, if using larger tomatoes, cut them into wedges. Put them in a 3-quart microwavable casserole. Add the onion, celery, chicken broth, tomato paste and basil.

Cook, uncovered, on High (100 percent) for 20 minutes. Stir in the salt and season to taste with pepper. Strain the soup to remove the tomato skins and seeds.

Serve garnished with spoonfuls of yogurt or sour cream, or stir in the heavy cream.

CHAPTER 3

POTATOES AND OTHER ROOT VEGETABLES

We eat potatoes by the bushel. Baked, fried, hashed and mashed, they are American favorites and figure in almost every regional cuisine. In fact, potatoes and other root vegetables are so commonplace that we often take them for granted. But we should not. They are rich in vitamins and minerals, not nearly as high in calories as we sometimes think, and tasty enough to stand up to other ingredients without overpowering them.

Using a microwave to cook root vegetables is a good idea. The time is shortened, it is true, but there are other major advantages too—no need to immerse the vegetables in water (and rob them of nutrients), or fry them in oil (and add calories) or bake them for a long time (and risk drying them out). The microwave cooks potatoes, sweet potatoes, carrots and other root vegetables in minutes without added fats or water, and leaves them moist, tender and bursting with steamy flavor. What could be better?

Watercress and Potato Soup

Serves 4

The peppery flavor of watercress combines well with potatoes to make this smooth, creamy soup. Serve it hot or chilled—it is delicious either way.

1 bunch watercress
2 tablespoons (1 ounce) butter
1 onion, finely chopped
1 stalk celery, chopped
2 medium-size potatoes, peeled and diced
3 cups chicken broth
1 tablespoon lemon juice
½ teaspoon salt
Pepper
½ cup heavy cream

Wash the watercress thoroughly. Reserve ½ cup of the leaves for garnish and chop the remaining leaves and stems into small pieces.

Put the butter in a 2-quart microwavable casserole and microwave on High (100 percent) for 20 seconds. Add the onion and celery and microwave, uncovered, on High (100 percent) for 2 to 3 minutes until the onion softens. Add the chopped watercress, potatoes, chicken broth, lemon juice, salt and pepper. Cover and microwave on High (100 percent) for 15 to 18 minutes until the potatoes are tender.

Transfer the soup to a blender or food processor and puree until smooth. Return the puree to the casserole and stir in the cream. Microwave on High (100 percent) for 2 minutes, until the soup is very hot. Garnish with the reserved watercress leaves just before serving.

Use the microwave to precook potatoes, turnips and rutabagas quickly for mashed and pureed dishes.

Potatoes au Gratin

Serves 4 to 6

A warming dish for a winter's day, and one that can be prepared in a fraction of the time required with conventional cooking.

> *4 medium-size potatoes*
> *4 tablespoons (2 ounces) butter or margarine*
> *¼ cup all-purpose flour*
> *1 small clove garlic, finely chopped*
> *⅛ teaspoon pepper*
> *1 teaspoon salt*
> *2 cups milk*
> *1 cup cheddar cheese*
> *¼ teaspoon paprika*

Scrub the potatoes and prick them with a fork. Microwave on High (100 percent) for 12 to 13 minutes.

Put the butter and garlic in a 1-quart glass measure. Microwave on High (100 percent) for 1½ minutes. Whisk in the flour, pepper and salt.

Put the milk in a 2-cup glass measure. Microwave on High (100 percent) for 3 minutes. Stir the hot milk into the flour mixture. Microwave on High (100 percent) for 2 minutes. Stir, and microwave on Medium (50 percent) for 2 minutes. Stir in the cheese.

Peel and slice the potatoes and arrange them in an 8-by-8-by-2-inch microwavable casserole. Pour the sauce over the potatoes, stirring until the potatoes are coated. Sprinkle with the paprika. Microwave on Medium (50 percent) for 5 to 7 minutes until the potatoes are tender.

Potato Boats

Serves 6

> 6 large baking potatoes
> 2 tablespoons (1 ounce) butter
> ½ teaspoon dried thyme, crushed
> 11-ounce can condensed cheddar cheese soup
> 2 tablespoons chopped parsley
> Ground nutmeg

Scrub the potatoes and prick them with a fork. Arrange the potatoes in a 12-by-8-inch microwavable casserole and microwave on High (100 percent) for 20 to 25 minutes, until they are almost done. Turn the potatoes and rotate the dish after 10 to 12 minutes. Let the potatoes stand, covered, for 5 to 10 minutes.

Cut the tops off the potatoes and scoop out the pulp, leaving a thin shell. Mash the potato pulp with the butter and crushed thyme. Gradually add the cheese soup and the parsley and beat the mixture until it is light and fluffy. Spoon the mixture back into the potato shells and sprinkle with nutmeg.

Return the stuffed potatoes to the same pan and microwave on High (100 percent) for 7 to 10 minutes, until they are hot. Rearrange after 3 to 4 minutes.

BAKING POTATOES

Baking a potato in the microwave takes mere minutes. Puncture it a few times, lay it on a paper towel and microwave on High (100 percent) for 6 to 8 minutes for a medium-size potato, a minute or two longer for a large potato. Increase the time slightly for each additional potato. However, if you plan to bake more than 4 or 5 large potatoes, you will do well to use a conventional oven—it will take about the same length of time.

Sweet and Sour Carrots

Serves 8

A cold, tangy carrot salad that gets better the longer it marinates—expressly designed for the plan-ahead cook or the late-night snacker.

> *1 pound carrots, cut into ⅛-inch rounds (about 4 cups)*
> *½ cup chopped green pepper*
> *¼ cup chopped yellow pepper*
> *7-ounce can tomato soup, undiluted*
> *¼ cup honey*
> *¼ cup cider vinegar*
> *¼ cup vegetable oil*
> *½ teaspoon dry mustard*
> *½ teaspoon Worcestershire sauce*

Put the carrots in a 2-quart microwavable casserole. Sprinkle with 2 tablespoons of water. Cover and microwave on High (100 percent) for 5 to 6 minutes, stirring every 2 minutes, until just tender. Drain the carrots and set them aside to cool.

Combine the cooled carrots with the peppers in a covered container.

Combine the tomato soup, honey, vinegar, oil, mustard and Worcestershire sauce in a microwavable bowl. Microwave on High (100 percent) for 2 to 3 minutes until bubbly. Allow to cool.

Pour the marinade over the chilled carrots and peppers. Cover and chill for several hours or up to a few days to allow the flavor to develop.

Twice-Baked Sweet Potatoes

Serves 4

You can prepare these buttery stuffed sweet potatoes hours before the second cooking. Just be sure to increase the time in the microwave by a minute or two to insure that they are heated through.

> *2 sweet potatoes, about 1 to 1¼ pounds*
> *1 tablespoon (½ ounce) butter*
> *1½ teaspoons brown sugar*
> *¼ teaspoon cinnamon*
> *¼ cup miniature marshmallows*

Scrub the sweet potatoes and prick them with a fork. Microwave on High (100 percent) for 8 to 9 minutes, turning after 4½ minutes. Remove the potatoes from the microwave and let them stand, covered, for 10 minutes.

Cut the potatoes in half lengthwise. Scoop out the pulp, leaving a ¼-inch shell. Mash the pulp and mix it with the butter, brown sugar and cinnamon until smooth. Spoon the mixture back into the shells. Top with the marshmallows, pressing them firmly into the filling.

Arrange the potatoes in an 8-by-8-by-2-inch microwavable dish. Microwave on High (100 percent) for 3 to 4 minutes until heated through.

Pineapple-Glazed Carrots

Serves 6

Sugar and spice and all that's nice make these carrots tasty—and cooking them in a microwavable bag is both handy and convenient.

> 1 tablespoon cornstarch
> ⅓ cup packed brown sugar
> ⅛ teaspoon ground nutmeg
> 1 cup pineapple juice
> 1 pound carrots, peeled and cut into ¼-inch diagonal slices
> 4 tablespoons (2 ounces) butter, cut into pieces

Shake the cornstarch, brown sugar and nutmeg in a 10-by-16-inch cooking bag, then set this in a 12-by-8-by-2-inch microwavable casserole. Add the pineapple juice and squeeze the bag gently to distribute the ingredients. Add the carrots and the butter pieces. Seal the bag securely and cut 6 ½-inch slits in the top.

Microwave on High (100 percent) for 20 to 22 minutes, until the carrots are tender. Rotate the casserole several times during cooking. Stir and serve.

JERUSALEM ARTICHOKES

Also known as sunchokes, these knobby little root vegetables are native to America, which makes their name something of a mystery. It may be derived from the Italian *girasole,* sunflower, to which they are related. They are totally *un*related to the better-known globe artichokes and are less widely available, although you will be able to find them in larger supermarkets and at specialty produce stores.

Jerusalem Artichoke Soup

Serve 6

A puree of Jerusalem artichokes forms the base for this richly satisfying, slightly lemony creamed soup.

> *1 pound Jerusalem artichokes*
> *1 tablespoon lemon juice*
> *3 cups chicken broth*
> *2 tablespoons (1 ounce) butter*
> *2 tablespoons all-purpose flour*
> *1 cup milk*
> *1 cup light cream*
> *1 teaspoon salt*
> *Pepper*
> *½ cup grated parmesan cheese*

Peel the artichokes and cut the larger ones so that the pieces are as uniform as possible. Put them in a 2-quart microwavable casserole and add the lemon juice and sufficient water to cover. Cover and microwave on High (100 percent) for 15 to 17 minutes, until very tender.

Drain the artichokes in a colander and put them in a food processor or blender. Add 1 cup of chicken broth and puree until smooth.

Put the butter in the casserole and microwave on High (100 percent) for 30 seconds. Stir in the flour. Stir in the remaining chicken broth, the artichoke puree, milk and cream. Season with salt and pepper to taste. Microwave, uncovered, on High (100 percent) for 6 to 7 minutes, until heated through.

Sprinkle with parmesan cheese before serving.

Gingered Vegetables

Serves 8

A hint of ginger adds zest to this vegetable medley.

> *1 pound carrots, sliced into ¼-inch rounds*
> *1 pound cauliflower, separated into florets*
> *1 tablespoon (½ ounce) butter*
> *¼ teaspoon ground nutmeg*
> *1 teaspoon salt*
> *1 teaspoon powdered ginger*
> *1 green pepper, stemmed, seeded and cut into strips*
> *1 medium-size zucchini (about 5 ounces) cut into*
>   *¼-inch rounds*
> *1 tablespoon lemon juice*

Combine the carrots and cauliflower in a 4-quart microwavable casserole. Dot with the butter. Sprinkle with the nutmeg, salt and ginger and mix. Cover and microwave on High (100 percent) for 12 minutes, stirring twice.

Add the green pepper and the zucchini. Microwave on High (100 percent) for 3 minutes until the vegetables are crisp-tender.

Sprinkle with lemon juice before serving.

CHAPTER 4

SQUASHES

By the end of the summer, the markets, roadside stands and greengrocers' produce counters are full to overflowing with squashes of every description. First come the summer squashes—green zucchini and yellow with its crooked neck. A little later in the fall acorn squash, spaghetti squash and butternut arrive. Nearly all are available at other times of the year, too, but never are they as wonderful as when they first appear in the late summer and fall.

Being watery vegetables, squashes do especially well in the microwave. They can be cooked whole (pierce them first with a sharp knife) or sliced—either way they are tender and juicy, full of flavor and ready to be blended with other vegetables and herbs or topped with creamy, rich cheese sauces.

Vegetable Platter

Serves 8 to 10

Make sure all the vegetables, except the asparagus, are of equal size before steaming them under dampened paper towels. This method cooks the vegetables perfectly with no added fat or seasoning. Eat them plain or let them cool and toss them with a vinaigrette for a delightfully cool summer salad.

> *16 asparagus stalks, trimmed*
> *½ cup ¼-inch slices zucchini*
> *½ cup ¼-inch slices yellow squash*
> *1½ cups julienned carrots*
> *½ cup halved brussels sprouts*
> *½ cup broccoli florets*
> *½ cup ¼-inch slices green pepper*
> *½ cup cauliflower florets*
> *¼ cup water*

Arrange the asparagus spears, tips pointing in, in the center of a microwavable platter. Position the zucchini and yellow squash around the asparagus. Arrange the carrots, brussels sprouts, broccoli, green pepper and cauliflower around the squash.

Sprinkle the vegetables with the water. Wet 3 sheets of paper towels under running water. (They should be soaked but not dripping.) Lay the wet towels over the vegetables.

Microwave on High (100 percent) for 9 to 15 minutes, or until crisp-tender. Rotate the platter twice during the cooking time. Pierce the vegetables with a fork to test for doneness—they should be soft and pliable. Let stand for 5 minutes before serving.

Stuffed Zucchini

Serves 2

There are endless ways to prepare zucchini and this is one of the simplest and best. Make this at the end of the summer when the garden is overflowing with zucchini, vine-ripened tomatoes and fresh basil.

> 2 slices bacon, cut into small pieces
> 1 medium-size zucchini (about 7 ounces)
> 1 scallion, thinly sliced
> ¼ cup chopped tomatoes
> 2 tablespoons dried bread crumbs
> ⅛ teaspoon pepper
> 1 teaspoon chopped fresh basil or ¼ teaspoon dried
> 2 tablespoons grated cheddar cheese

When zucchini reach huge proportions—as they often do by the end of the summer—they are best suited for stuffing rather than slicing and cooking any other way.

Lay the bacon on several layers of paper towels and microwave on High (100 percent) for 3 to 3½ minutes until crisp. Crumble the bacon when cool.

Cut the zucchini in half lengthwise. Scoop out the pulp, leaving a ¼-inch shell. Chop the zucchini pulp and combine it with the scallion, tomato, bread crumbs, pepper, basil and bacon. Stuff the zucchini shells with the mixture.

Put the stuffed shells in an 8-by-8-by-2-inch microwavable baking dish. Microwave on High (100 percent) for 5 to 6 minutes until the zucchini is tender. Top with grated cheese and microwave on High (100 percent) for 1 minute more to melt the cheese.

Spaghetti Squash with Vegetable and Cheese Sauce

Serves 4

Spaghetti squash is fun to serve—when you cut it open, the stringy pulp resembles cooked pasta. Cooked in the microwave until tender and then topped with a full-flavored cheese sauce, this dish is a robust main course.

>*2 pounds spaghetti squash*
>*1 tablespoon (½ ounce) butter*
>*1½ cups sliced mushrooms*
>*1 clove garlic, finely chopped*
>*1 cup bite-sized zucchini sticks*
>*2 scallions, thinly sliced*
>*1 tablespoon all-purpose flour*
>*½ cup milk*
>*⅛ teaspoon pepper*
>*½ cup ricotta cheese*
>*½ cup grated Swiss cheese*
>*2 tablespoons parmesan cheese*

Cut the squash into rings. Place in a large microwavable baking dish and cover with ¼ cup water. Microwave, covered, on High (100 percent) for 8 to 10 minutes, rotating the dish a quarter turn every 2 minutes, until the squash is tender. Let stand, covered, for 5 minutes.

While the squash is standing, put the butter in a 1-quart microwavable bowl. Microwave on High (100 percent) for 30 seconds until melted. Stir in the mushrooms and garlic. Microwave on High (100 percent) for 1½ to 2 minutes. Add the zucchini and scallions and microwave on High (100 percent) for 1½ to 2 minutes.

Add the flour and stir until it is well blended. Stir in the milk. Microwave on High (100 percent) for 2 to 3 minutes, stirring after 1½ minutes, until the sauce is thickened and bubbly. Stir in the pepper.

Add the cheeses one at a time, stirring well after each addition. Microwave on High (100 percent) for 1 to 2 minutes to heat the sauce through.

Shred the cooked squash, using 2 forks, and discard the seeds and skin. Divide the squash among 4 plates, spoon the sauce over it and serve immediately.

Garlic Baby Squash

Serves 2 to 4

Young tender squash will cook to succulent perfection in a dampened paper towel pouch in the microwave.

> *½ pound baby zucchini, cut in half diagonally*
> *½ pound baby yellow squash, cut in half*
> *   diagonally*
> *1 small carrot, thinly sliced*
> *1 clove garlic, finely chopped*
> *2 tablespoons (1 ounce) butter, cut into small pieces*
> *⅓ cup water*

Put a sheet of paper towel on a microwavable plate. Arrange the zucchini, squash, carrot and garlic in the center of the sheet and dot with butter. Fold the corners of the towel over the vegetables and cover with another sheet of paper towel. Fold the corners under. Pour the water evenly over the packet.

Microwave on High (100 percent) for 4½ to 6½ minutes, or until the vegetables are crisp-tender, rotating the plate once during cooking.

Remove from the oven and let stand for 2 minutes before serving.

Baby vegetables are becoming increasingly available in green-grocers' and even supermarkets. They simply are immature vegetables, picked very young when they are especially tender.

Sweet and Spicy Acorn Squash

Serves 2

Here is one of the easiest and most delicious ways to prepare acorn squash—every bite is sweet, juicy and tender.

A 3/4- to 1-pound acorn squash is large enough to serve 2 people as a side dish.

> *1 acorn squash*
> *2 tablespoons brown sugar*
> *1 tablespoon honey*
> *2 teaspoons butter*
> *⅛ teaspoon cinnamon*
> *Pinch of ground nutmeg*

Puncture the acorn squash in 2 places with a sharp knife. Put the squash in a microwavable dish and microwave on High (100 percent) for 7 to 8 minutes, turning it over after 3½ to 4 minutes.

Remove the squash from the microwave and allow it to stand for 5 minutes. Cut it in half and scrape out the seeds.

Put 1 tablespoon of brown sugar, 1½ teaspoons of honey and 1 teaspoon of butter in each squash cavity. Cover with transparent wrap and microwave on High (100 percent) for 2 to 3 minutes until the squash is tender and the filling is bubbling.

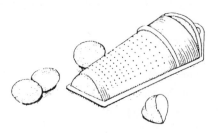

Honey-Glazed Squash

Serves 6

A pleasant and unusual way to serve acorn squash or one of the other hard-skinned squashes.

> 2 acorn squashes
> 1 cup chicken broth
> ¼ cup honey
> 2 teaspoons cornstarch
> 1 teaspoon grated orange rind
> ½ teaspoon powdered ginger
> Raisins, for garnish

Puncture each squash in 2 places with a sharp knife. Place them in a microwavable dish and microwave on High (100 percent) for 7 to 8 minutes, turning them over after 3½ to 4 minutes.

Remove the squashes from the microwave and allow to stand for 5 minutes. Peel and seed the squashes and cut them into ½-inch slices.

Combine the chicken broth, honey, cornstarch, orange rind and ginger in a 3-quart microwavable casserole. Microwave on High (100 percent) for 4 minutes or until boiling and thickened, stirring twice. Add the squash slices. Cover and microwave on High (100 percent) for 4 to 8 minutes until the squash is glazed, stirring every 2 minutes. Serve topped with raisins.

Summer Squash au Gratin

Serves 6

Yellow squash is frequently called summer squash. This recipe is just as good made with zucchini.

> 3½ cups sliced yellow squash (about 2½ medium-size squash)
> ¾ cup toasted whole wheat bread crumbs
> 1¼ cups grated Swiss cheese
> ½ teaspoon salt
> ½ teaspoon pepper

Arrange a layer of squash slices in the bottom of an 8-by-8-by-2-inch microwavable baking dish. Sprinkle a third of the bread crumbs, cheese, salt and pepper over the squash. Repeat the layering process 2 more times, ending with a layer of the cheese.

Microwave on Medium (50 percent) for 10 to 12 minutes, rotating the dish a quarter turn every 2 minutes until the cheese is bubbly and the squash tender. Allow to stand for 3 minutes before serving.

Vegetable Pasta Carbonara

Serves 4-6

> 1 cup ½-inch pieces yellow squash
> 1 cup 1-inch pieces asparagus
> 1½ cups small cauliflower florets
> 1 cup thinly sliced carrots
> 3 tablespoons (1½ ounces) butter

2 cloves garlic, finely chopped
3 large eggs
1 pound hot, cooked linguine, drained
5 ounces parmesan cheese, grated
¼ cup heavy cream
10 slices bacon, cooked and crumbled
¼ cup chopped parsley
½ teaspoon pepper

Put the squash in the center of a 12-inch microwavable plate. Arrange the asparagus on the plate in a ring around the squash. Combine the cauliflower and carrots and distribute in a ring around the asparagus.

Put the butter and garlic in a 1-cup glass measure and microwave on High (100 percent) for 30 seconds, until the butter is melted. Spoon the garlic butter evenly over the vegetables.

Cover the vegetables with heavy-duty transparent wrap, leaving one corner open to vent. Microwave on High (100 percent) for 6 to 8 minutes, until the vegetables are crisp-tender, rotating the plate once during cooking. Remove them from the oven and let stand for 2 minutes.

Beat the eggs well in a large bowl. Add the hot linguine to the eggs and toss well. Add the cooked vegetables. Set aside ¼ cup of the cheese and add the remaining cheese to the bowl along with the cream, bacon, parsley and pepper. Toss well and serve with the reserved cheese on the side.

CHAPTER 5

BEANS AND LEGUMES

R obust and filling, beans and legumes have long been relegated to the ranks of "peasant" food. With the heightened interest in down-home fare and the popularity of Tex-Mex and Mexican cooking, they have recently become quite fashionable. But in vogue or not, they have always been delicious.

Legumes technically means any member of the pea family, such as peas, beans, lentils, peanuts, alfalfa, and many, many more. But we usually apply it to mean dried beans and peas of all descriptions.

All the recipes in this chapter that call for canned beans can be made with dried beans that have been soaked first—either overnight in enough water to cover, or by the microwave methods described here.

Whether you use dried, canned or frozen beans, their distinctive flavor and texture are so appealing that you will find these dishes quickly becoming part of your regular repertoire.

Rocky Mountain Bean Casserole

Serves 8 to 10

This substantial bean casserole keeps for several days in the refrigerator and will round out any meal from a simple lunch to a late-night supper.

> *12 ounces dried Great Northern or kidney beans*
> *6 cups water*
> *1 onion, finely chopped*
> *4 strips cooked bacon, crumbled*
> *2 teaspoons salt*
> *Pepper*
> *2 tablespoons brown sugar*
> *1 teaspoon dry mustard*

Pick through dried beans, discarding broken beans and any stray stones or other debris. Rinse them thoroughly under running water before soaking.

Rinse the beans thoroughly and put them in a 3-quart microwavable casserole. Add 3 cups of water, cover and microwave on High (100 percent) for 10 to 15 minutes, until boiling. Stir the beans and let stand, covered, for at least 1 hour. Drain in a colander.

Return the drained beans to the casserole. Add the remaining 3 cups of water, the onion, bacon, salt and pepper. Cover and microwave on High (100 percent) for 12 to 15 minutes, until boiling. Stir the beans, cover again and cook on Medium (50 percent) for 35 to 50 minutes, until the beans are tender, stirring after 10 minutes. Let stand, covered, for 5 minutes.

Stir in the brown sugar and dry mustard. Cover and microwave on Medium (50 percent) for 1½ minutes, stirring after 45 seconds.

Cheesy Refried Beans

Serves 6 to 8

Refried beans are the expected side dish at nearly any Mexican or Tex-Mex meal, but the smooth mash of beans flavored with onions and garlic is good at nearly any meal. If you do not have Monterey jack cheese on hand, substitute cheddar.

No need to soak dried beans overnight when you have a microwave. "Soaking" in the microwave takes only 15 minutes followed by an hour's standing time. The beans are then ready to cook.

> *2 cups dried kidney or pinto beans*
> *6 cups water*
> *3 medium-size onions*
> *Salt and pepper*
> *2 tablespoons butter*
> *2 cloves garlic, finely chopped*
> *1½ cups Monterey jack cheese*

Rinse the beans thoroughly and put them in a 3-quart microwavable casserole. Add 3 cups of water, cover and microwave on High (100 percent) for 10 to 15 minutes, until boiling. Stir the beans and let stand, covered, for at least 1 hour.

Halve each of the onions. Chop one half finely, cover, and set aside.

Drain the beans in a colander and return the beans to the casserole. Add the remaining 3 cups of water and the 5 onion halves and season with salt and pepper. Cover and microwave on High (100 percent) for 12 to 15 minutes, until boiling. Stir the beans, cover again and cook on Medium (50 percent) for 35 to 50 minutes, until the beans are tender, stirring after 10 minutes. Let stand, covered, for 5 minutes. Drain the beans in a colander, reserving the cooking liquid. Remove and discard the onions.

Put the beans in a bowl, add ¼ cup of the reserved cooking liquid, discarding the rest. Mash the beans thoroughly.

Combine the butter with the chopped onion and garlic in a 1-cup glass measure. Microwave on High (100 percent) for 3 to 4 minutes, until the butter is melted and the onion is softened.

Add the butter-onion mixture to the mashed beans and season with salt and pepper. Transfer the beans to a shallow 10-inch microwavable dish. Top with the grated cheese and microwave on Medium (50 percent) for 2 to 4 minutes, until the cheese is melted.

Split Pea Soup

Serves 6 to 8

Thick, aromatic split pea soup is a warming and comforting dish for a cold winter day or a chilly spring evening.

> *1 cup dried green split peas*
> *5 cups chicken broth*
> *½ cup chopped celery*
> *½ cup chopped onion*
> *½ cup chopped potato*
> *¼ cup chopped ham*
> *½ teaspoon dried thyme*

Rinse and drain the peas and put them in a 3-quart microwavable casserole. Add the chicken broth, celery, onion, potato, ham and thyme. Cover and microwave on High (100 percent) for 10 minutes.

Stir the soup, replace the cover and microwave on Medium (50 percent) for 60 to 70 minutes, stirring every 30 minutes. Let stand, covered, for 10 minutes before serving.

When cooking beans, cover the casserole with a tight-fitting lid. Transparent wrap may not hold up to long cooking and if it splits, too much moisture will escape.

Lentil Soup

Serves 6

A lot of ingredients plus very little fuss add up to a tasty, hearty soup.

Beans and legumes are excellent— not to mention economical— sources of protein.

1¼ cups lentils, washed and drained
5 cups water
¾ cup chopped carrots
½ cup chopped celery
½ cup chopped onion
3 slices bacon, cut into small pieces
2 cloves garlic, finely chopped
1 bay leaf
3 tablespoons chopped parsley
1 teaspoon salt
½ teaspoon dried thyme
½ teaspoon dried tarragon
⅛ teaspoon dried oregano
⅛ teaspoon pepper
16-ounce can tomatoes, chopped, juice reserved

Put the lentils, water, carrots, celery, onion, bacon, garlic and bay leaf in a 3½-quart microwavable casserole. Cover and microwave on High (100 percent) for 15 minutes, stirring after 8 minutes.

Stir in the parsley, salt, thyme, tarragon, oregano and pepper. Cover and microwave on High (100 percent) for 5 minutes. Stir in the tomatoes and the reserved juice. Continue microwaving, covered, on High (100 percent) for 20 to 25 minutes, stirring every 5 minutes, until the lentils and vegetables are tender. Remove the bay leaf before serving.

Red River Chili

Serves 6 to 8

How could a chapter on beans not include chili? This one is nice and hot, full-bodied and rich.

½ pound ground pork
½ pound ground beef
2 medium-size onions, chopped
1 green pepper, chopped
3 garlic cloves, finely chopped
16-ounce can crushed tomatoes, including juice
8-ounce can tomato sauce
3 tablespoons chili powder
12-ounce can tomato juice
1 cup water
2 teaspoons dried basil
1 teaspoon salt
1 tablespoon paprika
16-ounce can pinto or kidney beans, drained

Put the pork, beef, onion, pepper and garlic in a 3-quart microwavable casserole. Blend together with a fork or your fingers. Cover and microwave on High (100 percent) for 8 to 10 minutes. Drain off the excess liquid.

Add the tomatoes, tomato sauce, chili powder, tomato juice, water, basil, salt and paprika. Cover and microwave on Medium (50 percent) for 30 to 35 minutes, stirring after 15 minutes.

Add the beans and stir well. Cover and microwave on Medium (50 percent) for 8 to 10 minutes. Let stand, covered, for 5 to 10 minutes before serving.

After you have made a chili recipe that you like, improvise and invent your own particular stew. Add as much "heat" as you and your family can take.

Boston Baked Beans

Serves 6 to 8

The classic version of this dish calls for a lengthy cook-ing time, but this recipe made in the microwave is ideal for the cook in a hurry.

>   2 15-ounce cans pinto beans, drained
>   ⅓ cup packed brown sugar
>   ⅓ cup molasses
>   2 teaspoons dry mustard
>   1 medium-size onion, cut into 8 pieces
>   3 slices bacon, cut into ½-inch pieces
>   2 teaspoons cornstarch

Beans continue to absorb liquid during standing time.

Combine the beans, brown sugar, molasses and mus-tard in a 2-quart microwavable casserole. Stir in the onion and bacon and cover. Microwave on High (100 percent) for 12 to 14 minutes, stirring every 4 minutes.

Mix the cornstarch with 1 tablespoon of water to make a smooth paste and stir this into the bean mixture. Cover and microwave on High (100 percent) for 2 to 3 minutes until thickened and bubbly. Allow to stand, covered, for 5 minutes before serving.

Winter Succotash

Serves 8

A slightly more traditional succotash uses only lima beans and corn, but adding carrots gives the familiar dish color, texture and improved flavor.

> *10-ounce package frozen carrots*
> *10-ounce package frozen lima beans*
> *10-ounce package frozen whole kernel corn*
> *⅓ cup half-and-half*
> *4 tablespoons (2 ounces) butter*
> *1 teaspoon dried thyme*
> *1 tablespoon chopped parsley*
> *1 teaspoon salt*
> *Pepper*

Combine the carrots, lima beans and corn in a 2-quart microwavable casserole. Cover and microwave on High (100 percent) for 9 to 12 minutes or until the vegetables have completely thawed and are tender, stirring after 4½ minutes.

Add the half-and-half, butter, thyme, salt and pepper and stir to combine. Cover and cook on High (100 percent) for 2 to 4 minutes or until heated through.

CHAPTER 6

VEGETABLE SOUPS AND CASSEROLES

We love to serve soups and casseroles. They combine so many of our favorite flavors and ingredients while appealing to our sense of well-being and comfort. What is more, many can be prepared in advance of mealtime—a bonus for the busy cook and homemaker.

Before the advent of microwave cooking, making soup was frequently an all-day task. Long, slow cooking was needed to soften the vegetables and develop their flavors. With a microwave, the vegetables soften and the flavors come out in a fraction of the time. The resulting soup is as tasty and satisfying as any made the old-fashioned way. The same is true of casseroles, many of which can be served as the main course accompanied by a simple green salad and a loaf of warm bread.

Don't forget! Microwaving is a great way to cook in summer—or any other time—without heating up the kitchen.

Corn Chowder

Serves 6 to 8

Even in the bleakest winter you can make this creamy corn chowder, using canned or frozen (and completely thawed) corn. Add extra pepper for sharper flavor.

> *4 slices bacon*
> *1 cup diced ham*
> *¾ cup chopped onion*
> *½ teaspoon finely chopped garlic*
> *2 cups water*
> *1½ cups diced potatoes*
> *½ teaspoon salt*
> *¼ teaspoon pepper*
> *16-ounces cream-style corn*
> *8-ounces whole kernel corn, drained*
> *½ cup half-and-half*

Lay the bacon on several layers of paper towels and cover with a paper towel. Microwave on High (100 percent) for 2 to 2½ minutes until crisp and browned.

Crumble the bacon into a 2½ quart microwavable casserole. Add the ham, onion and garlic. Microwave on High (100 percent) for 3 minutes until the onion is softened.

Stir in the water, potatoes, salt and pepper. Cover and microwave on High (100 percent) for 10 to 12 minutes, stirring every 4 minutes, until the potatoes are tender.

Add the creamed and whole corn and stir to blend. Microwave, covered, on High (100 percent) for 3 to 4 minutes, until boiling. Stir in the half-and-half. Microwave, covered, on High (100 percent) for 2 to 3 minutes until heated through. Take care not to let it boil.

Garden Soup

Serves 10

Just about everything good from the kitchen garden goes into this wholesome soup. Make a large batch and keep it in the refrigerator for several days—great for quick meals and after-school snacks.

1 tablespoon olive oil
1 medium-size onion, finely chopped
3 cloves garlic, finely chopped
1 teaspoon dried oregano
2 ripe tomatoes, peeled, seeded and chopped
2 tablespoons tomato paste
2 cups chopped potatoes
1 cup chopped carrots
1 cup chopped celery
1 cup shredded red cabbage
6 cups water
1 teaspoon salt
½ teaspoon pepper
1 cup chopped green beans
⅔ cup chopped zucchini
3 tablespoons finely chopped parsley
1 teaspoon dried basil
Parmesan cheese, grated

Onions and garlic are often microwaved in a glass measure before being added to the casserole or soup; this softens them and releases their superb flavors.

Combine the oil, onion, garlic and oregano in a 4-quart microwavable casserole. Cover and microwave on High (100 percent) for 2½ to 3 minutes until the onion is softened.

Stir in the tomatoes and tomato paste. Microwave, covered, on High (100 percent) for 2½ to 3 minutes. Stir in the potatoes, carrots, celery, cabbage, water, salt and pepper. Microwave on Medium (50 percent) for 35 to 40 minutes until the vegetables are almost tender.

Add the green beans and zucchini, cover and microwave on High (100 percent) for 10 minutes. Stir in the parsley and basil. Cover and microwave on High (100 percent) for 10 to 15 minutes until the soup is hot.

Pass a bowl of freshly grated parmesan at the table so that people can help themselves.

Creamy Broccoli Soup

Serves 4 to 5

This quickly made soup is just right for a weekend lunch or a simple supper. Fresh broccoli is readily available year round, which makes the soup even more appealing.

> 2 cups chopped celery
> 1 cup chopped onion
> 1 bunch fresh broccoli, trimmed and chopped
> 1½ cups chicken broth
> 1 cup cottage cheese
> 1 cup milk
> ⅛ teaspoon pepper
> ½ teaspoon dried thyme
> Pinch of ground allspice

Combine the celery, onion, broccoli and chicken broth in a 2½-quart microwavable casserole. Cover with transparent wrap and microwave on High (100 percent) for 15 minutes, stirring twice.

Turn the mixture into a blender or food processor, add the cottage cheese and process until smooth. Return the pureed mixture to the casserole. Stir in the milk, pepper, thyme and allspice. Microwave on High (100 percent) for 6 to 8 minutes, stirring after 3 to 4 minutes, until the soup is piping hot.

Vichyssoise

Serves 6

This delicately flavored cold soup was a instant success when a New York chef created it during the summer of 1910, and it has never lost its power to charm. If you are unable to obtain leeks, you can substitute three finely chopped onions.

Once considered exotic, leeks are now available nearly all year long. They tend to collect sand and grit in their tightly folded leaves, so be sure to wash them thoroughly.

> *4 medium-size potatoes (2 pounds), peeled and*
>   *chopped*
> *6 leeks*
> *6 cups hot chicken broth*
> *1 cup heavy cream*
> *1 teaspoon salt*
> *Chopped chives, for garnish*
> *Black pepper*

Put the potatoes in a 2-quart microwavable casserole. Slice the white part and the lower third of the green part of the leeks. Rinse thoroughly in cold running water and place in the casserole with the potatoes. Add the chicken broth.

Cover the casserole and microwave on High (100 percent) for 10 to 12 minutes, until the potatoes are very soft.

Puree the soup in a food processor or blender. Stir in the cream and the salt and chill for at least 4 hours before serving. Garnish with chopped chives and freshly ground black pepper.

Southern-Style Potato Corn Pudding

Serves 8

A hearty corn and potato casserole reminiscent of Southern spoon bread.

1 tablespoon (½ ounce) butter
1½ cups frozen Southern-style hash brown
    potatoes
2 scallions, sliced
8-ounce can kernel corn, drained
1 teaspoon salt
⅛ teaspoon dried thyme
⅛ teaspoon pepper
¾ cup milk
2 large eggs, well beaten
¼ teaspoon paprika

Put the butter in a 9-inch microwavable round casserole and microwave on High (100 percent) for 30 seconds, until melted.

Stir in the potatoes and scallions. Microwave on High (100 percent) for 3½ to 4½ minutes until the scallions soften.

Stir in the corn, salt, thyme, pepper, milk and eggs. Microwave on High (100 percent) for 4 minutes, stirring thoroughly after 2 minutes. Sprinkle with paprika. Microwave on Medium (50 percent) for 5 to 7 minutes, rotating the dish a quarter turn every 2½ minutes, until the center is set.

Allow to stand for 5 minutes before serving.

Corn kernels are often used in microwave cooking because they are uniform in size and they cook evenly. Defrosted frozen corn can be substituted for fresh—and vice versa.

Rice Pilaf

Serves 6 to 8

Crunchy sliced almonds turn this colorful rice pilaf into something quite special.

>   *3 tablespoons (1½ ounces) butter*
>   *1 cup long grain rice*
>   *⅓ cup sliced almonds*
>   *2 cups beef broth, boiling hot*
>   *½ teaspoon salt (optional)*
>   *1 cup frozen peas*
>   *1 cup grated carrots*

Put the butter in a 2½-quart microwavable casserole and microwave on High (100 percent) for 30 seconds.

Add the rice and the almonds and stir to coat with the butter. Microwave on High (100 percent) for 4 minutes, stirring twice. The rice will be golden brown. Add the boiling broth and salt (if needed) and stir. Microwave, covered, on High (100 percent) for 2 minutes. Microwave, still covered, on Medium (50 percent) for 15 to 18 minutes, until the rice is cooked.

Put the peas in a 2-cup glass measure. Microwave, covered, on High (100 percent) for 3 minutes.

Add the peas and carrots to the rice. Stir to combine and serve immediately.

Broccoli Cheese Casserole

Serves 6 to 8

Broccoli casserole with a smooth cheese sauce has long been a popular side dish for buffets and family suppers.

> 2 large bunches broccoli, with thickest parts of stems removed
> ½ cup chopped onion
> 3 large eggs
> ½ cup small curd cottage cheese
> 2 cups grated Monterey jack cheese
> ½ cup grated cheddar cheese
> ½ cup half-and-half
> 1 tablespoon finely chopped parsley

Wash the broccoli, cut it into bite-sized pieces and put it in a 2-quart microwavable casserole. Cover and microwave on High (100 percent) for 3 to 3½ minutes, stirring after 2 minutes. Remove from the microwave.

Put the onion in a 1-cup glass measure. Microwave on High (100 percent) for 1 minute until softened.

Beat the eggs in a large bowl. Stir in the cottage, jack and cheddar cheeses, half-and-half, softened onion and parsley. Add the broccoli and stir to combine.

Pour into a 2½-quart round microwavable casserole. Microwave on Medium (50 percent) for 15 to 18 minutes, stirring once, until the broccoli is tender and the cheeses are melted.

Monterey Jack Casserole

Serves 4

Smooth-melting Monterey jack cheese combines with wild rice, tomatoes, zucchini and sour cream in a filling, tasty casserole you can serve either as a side dish or the main course.

If you assemble a casserole well ahead of serving, increase the heating time by several minutes before taking it to the table.

> ½ pound Monterey jack cheese
> 2 cups cooked long grain and wild rice mix
> 3 tablespoons toasted bread crumbs
> 1 medium-size zucchini, sliced ⅛ inch thick
> 1 large tomato, thinly sliced
> 1 cup sour cream
> 1 small clove garlic, finely chopped
> 1 tablespoon finely chopped scallion
> 1 tablespoon finely chopped parsley

Thinly slice half of the cheese and grate the remainder. Set aside.

Spread the rice in the bottom of an 8-by-8-by-2-inch microwavable dish. Cover with the cheese slices. Sprinkle 1 tablespoon of the bread crumbs over the cheese. Cover with a layer of zucchini and sprinkle 1 tablespoon of bread crumbs on top. Cover with the tomato slices and sprinkle with the remaining bread crumbs.

Combine the sour cream, garlic, scallion and parsley. Spread the mixture over the tomatoes. Top with the grated cheese.

Microwave, covered, on Medium (50 percent) for 14 to 16 minutes, rotating the dish a quarter turn every 4 minutes, until the tomatoes and zucchini are tender.

CHAPTER 7

SAVORY SNACKS

L et's face it—we all love to snack. Some days the desire is greater than others, and sometimes we overindulge, but, there is no question that snacking is part of life, and a very pleasurable one. So it is far more sensible—and ultimately more satisfying—to munch on homemade snacks that taste good and are quickly made than to reach for a bag of potato chips or pretzels.

Not all the snacks in this chapter are low in calories, nor are they necessarily low in sodium, but they are high in flavor and goodness. Each one will quickly alleviate hungry cravings during those times when dinner is hours away and lunch is far behind us—or when we simply have no time to prepare a full meal.

Tote-Along Vegetables with Dill Dressing

Serves 2

A wet sheet of paper towel steams the vegetables without overcooking them and leaves their colors vivid. After the vegetables are wrapped in the towels, they can be stored in a plastic bag in the refrigerator. The dressing can also be prepared ahead of time.

> *1 medium-size carrot, peeled and cut into ¼-inch diagonal slices*
> *2 small heads broccoli, cut into florets*
> *½ medium-size zucchini, cut into ¼-inch rounds*
> *¼ medium-size yellow squash, cut into ¼-inch rounds*
> *¼ medium-size green pepper, cut into strips*
> *Garlic powder*
> *Pepper*
> *½ cup plain yogurt*
> *¼ teaspoon fresh dill*
> *¼ teaspoon freshly chopped chives*

Toss the vegetables together in a large bowl. Season to taste with the garlic powder and pepper.

Arrange the vegetables on a series of wet paper towels, leaving enough room so that you can fold each towel to form a pouch. Put the wrapped vegetables on a microwavable plate and microwave on High (100 percent) for 3 to 4 minutes, or until they all are tender.

Combine the yogurt, dill and chives in a bowl. Spoon the dressing over the vegetables and serve.

Take the wrapped vegetables to work with you and microwave them there.

Cheesy Bean Dip

Makes 1 1/2 cups

A spicy dip to serve hot with tortilla chips. If you make it ahead of time, reheat it in the microwave for three to four minutes.

15-ounce can red kidney beans, drained
1/4 cup finely chopped onion
1 clove garlic, finely chopped
3/4 cup grated sharp cheddar cheese
1/4 cup grated Monterey jack with jalapeño pepper
  cheese
2 teaspoons cider vinegar
1/4 teaspoon salt
1/4 teaspoon ground cumin
1/8 teaspoon pepper

Put the drained beans, onion and garlic in a 1 1/2-quart microwavable casserole. Cover and microwave on High (100 percent) for 4 to 5 minutes, stirring after 2 minutes, until the beans are hot.

Combine the hot beans with all the remaining ingredients in a blender or food processor. You may have to do this in several batches. Puree until the cheese blends in and the beans are quite smooth. Taste and adjust the seasoning if necessary.

Stuff pita bread pockets with the bean mixture and top with shredded lettuce and chopped tomatoes for an unusual but appealing sandwich.

Zesty Nacho Platter

Makes 1½ cups cheese sauce

Top your favorite cracker with cheese or a cheese spread and microwave on Medium (50 percent) for 2 to 3 minutes and you have an instant warm snack for unexpected cocktail guests.

When you want something cheesy and piquant, these nachos can be made in moments.

> *4 ounces cheddar cheese, grated*
> *1 ounce Monterey jack with jalapeño pepper cheese, grated*
> *¼ cup milk*
> *2 scallions, sliced*
> *1 tablespoon white wine*
> *Tortilla chips*
> *½ cup seeded, chopped cucumber*
> *1 tomato, seeded and chopped*

Combine the cheddar and jack cheeses with the milk, scallions and wine in a 4-cup microwavable measure. Microwave on Medium (50 percent) for 2 to 2½ minutes, stirring every minute, until the cheese is melted. Whisk until smooth.

Spread the tortilla chips on a serving platter. Pour the cheese sauce over the chips and top with the cucumber and tomato.

Pepperoni Pizzas

Makes 8

Leave off the pepperoni if you are watching calories and substitute chopped turkey or chicken.

> *1 cup grated mozzarella cheese*
> *1 cup pitted ripe olives*

½ pound pepperoni, chopped
½ cup mayonnaise
¼ teaspoon Italian seasoning
4 English muffins

Combine the mozzarella cheese, olives, pepperoni, mayonnaise and Italian seasoning in a mixing bowl. Stir well.

Split and toast the English muffins. Arrange them on a large microwavable platter. Distribute the topping evenly on the muffin halves.

Microwave on High (100 percent) for 2 minutes or until the cheese is melted. Serve at once.

Savory Add-A-Crunch

Makes about 3 cups

Adding wheat germ, bran or your favorite chopped nuts to this snack mixture makes it especially crunchy and immediately turns it into your own creation.

2 cups rolled oats
8 tablespoons (4 ounces) butter, melted
⅓ cup grated parmesan cheese
⅓ cup wheat germ, unprocessed bran or
   chopped nuts (optional)
¼ teaspoon onion or garlic salt

Combine all the ingredients thoroughly in an 11-by-7-inch microwavable baking dish and distribute well. Microwave on High (100 percent) for 8 to 9 minutes, until the mixture is a light golden brown. Stir the mixture after every 3 minutes of cooking. Cool and serve.

Hot Crab Spread

Makes 1½ cups

This is sure to be a hit at your next party. Serve it in a chafing dish or on a hot tray with rye cocktail bread or crackers.

> *8-ounce package cream cheese*
> *2 6-ounce cans crabmeat, drained and flaked*
> *¾ cup mayonnaise*
> *¼ cup white wine or dry vermouth*
> *2 tablespoons finely chopped onion*
> *2 tablespoons Dijon mustard*
> *½ teaspoon salt*
> *½ teaspoon chopped garlic*
> *⅛ teaspoon hot pepper sauce*

If you wrap bread in paper towels, it will reheat very nicely in the microwave without drying out.

Put the cream cheese in a 1½-quart microwavable casserole. Microwave on High (100 percent) for 45 to 60 seconds, until softened.

Stir in the crabmeat, mayonnaise, wine, onion, mustard, salt, garlic and hot pepper sauce. Microwave on High (100 percent) for 3½ to 4 minutes, until the mixture is hot and bubbly. Serve at once.

Pita Pocket Vegetable Melt

Serves 4

A vegetarian sandwich that will easily fill the gap between meals when a hearty but healthy snack is in order. This also makes a good lunch: fill the sandwich and carry it to the office to microwave there.

> ½ cup chopped onion
> 1 clove garlic, finely chopped
> ½ cup sliced mushrooms
> ½ cup cubed munster cheese
> 1 cup chopped tomato
> 2–3 tablespoons grated parmesan cheese
> 4 small pita pockets

Put the onion, garlic and mushrooms in a microwavable bowl and microwave on High for 2 to 3 minutes until the onions are softened and the mushrooms tender. Toss the mushroom mixture with the munster cheese and tomato, and sprinkle with the parmesan. Open the pita pockets and spoon an equal amount of filling into the pocket of each one.

Lay each sandwich on several layers of paper towel. Lay an additional paper towel over each and fold the corners under to make a package. Microwave the sandwiches on High for 1 to 2 minutes to warm them and allow the cheese to melt slightly. Serve warm.

Tuna Melt Croissants

Makes 2 sandwiches

> 6½-ounce can water-packed tuna, drained
> ½ cup chopped celery
> ½ cup chopped white onion
> 1 hard-cooked egg, finely chopped
> 1 scallion, finely chopped
> 1 tablespoon pickle relish
> ¼ cup mayonnaise
> Salt and pepper
> 2 croissants, sliced in half or 4 slices of bread
> 1 slice American cheese, cut into strips

To reduce the
sodium content of
this recipe, use
low-sodium tuna
and cheese and
eliminate the salt.

Combine the tuna, celery, onion, egg, scallion, relish and mayonnaise in a mixing bowl. Add salt and pepper to taste.

Cover the bottom half of each croissant with half the mixture. Top each portion with half the cheese strips and add the top halves of the croissants. Wrap each sandwich in a sheet of paper towel. Put the sandwiches on a microwavable plate and microwave on High (100 percent) for 45 seconds to 1 minute, until the cheese is melted and the tuna is thoroughly warmed.

CHAPTER 8

SWEET SNACKS

W hen you want something sweet, reach for a muffin or piece of banana bread. Or how about handful of caramel popcorn or crunchy granola? These are snacks that reassure the most active sweet tooth and yet do not overload our (or our children's) systems with too much sugar or preservatives.

Babies are born with a craving for sugar, so it is no surprise that at some point we all have an urge to eat sweet things. Fruit, nuts, coconut and several other foods are naturally sweet, and make attractive snacks on their own. But sometimes it is pleasant to ring the changes. The recipes here suggest some ways of coaxing them into even more satisfying snacks for after school, after work, after play, after supper—or *before* anything!

Create-A-Wholegrain Muffin

Makes about 18 muffins

Muffins bake
beautifully in the
microwave, when
you cook them in
batches, a few at a
time.

Bran and rolled oats combine with molasses and brown sugar for a dense, delicious any-time-of-day muffin.

¾ cup milk
¾ cup bran cereal
1 large egg
⅓ cup vegetable oil
¼ cup molasses or honey
¼ cup packed brown sugar
1 cup quick-cooking rolled oats
⅔ cup all-purpose flour
1 tablespoon baking powder
¼ teaspoon salt (optional)

Combine the milk and bran cereal in a medium-sized bowl. Add the egg, oil, molasses and brown sugar and mix well.

Combine the oats, flour, baking powder and salt in another bowl. Add to the milk mixture and mix just until the dry ingredients are moistened.

Line microwavable cupcake pans with paper liners. Half fill 6 or 7 with the batter and microwave on High for 1¾ minutes, or until a toothpick inserted into the center comes out clean. Rotate the muffin dish a quarter turn after 1 minute of cooking time. Immediately remove the muffins from the dish.

Half fill 6 or 7 more pans and repeat the process until all the batter is used.

Banana Nut Bread

Makes 16 2-inch squares

This excellent bread is cooked in just eight minutes.
Spread thinly with butter, the squares make a delicious
snack served with a glass of cold milk.

8 tablespoons (4 ounces) butter
¾ cup packed brown sugar
1 ripe banana, mashed
1 teaspoon lemon juice
2 large eggs
1¼ cups all-purpose flour
½ teaspoon baking powder
12 teaspoon baking soda
½ teaspoon salt
¼ teaspoon ground nutmeg
½ cup chopped pecans

Combine the butter and sugar in a mixing bowl. Stir
in the banana, lemon juice and eggs and mix well.

Sift together the flour, baking powder, baking soda,
salt and nutmeg in another bowl. Combine the mixtures, stirring until the flour is just incorporated, and
then stir in the pecans.

Line an 8-inch-square microwavable baking dish
with wax paper. Pour the batter into the dish and microwave on High (100 percent) for 7 to 9 minutes until
a toothpick inserted in the center comes out clean.
Rotate the dish a quarter turn every 2 minutes of cooking time. Remove the bread from the oven and let it rest
in the pan for another 5 minutes.

Turn the bread out onto a wire rack and let it cool
for 10 minutes. Peel off the wax paper and cut the bread
into 16 squares.

Bake quick breads
in the microwave
in dishes lined
with wax paper.
This prevents
them from
becoming soft on
the bottom.

Apricot-Zucchini Muffins

Makes about 18 muffins

Use the microwave to help shell nuts such as brazil nuts or walnuts, which are normally hard to shell without breaking. Put 8 ounces of nuts in a cup of water and microwave on High (100 percent) for 4 to 5 minutes. Now shell them.

Plenty of wholesome ingredients go into making these sweet, crumb-topped muffins—but they take only minutes to mix and bake.

1 large egg
¼ cup sugar
½ cup plus 3 tablespoons packed brown sugar
½ cup vegetable oil
½ cup mashed canned apricots
½ teaspoon vanilla extract
¼ teaspoon almond extract
¾ cup whole wheat flour
¾ cup plus 3 tablespoons all-purpose flour
1 teaspoon cinnamon
½ teaspoon salt
½ teaspoon ground nutmeg
1 teaspoon baking soda
½ cup chopped dates
1 cup grated zucchini
3 tablespoons quick-cooking rolled oats
3 tablespoon chopped walnuts
3 tablespoons (1½ ounces) butter

Stir together the egg, sugar, ½ cup of the brown sugar, oil, apricots, vanilla and almond extracts.

Combine the whole wheat flour, ¾ cup of the all-purpose flour, ¾ teaspoon of cinnamon, and the salt, nutmeg, baking soda, baking powder and dates. Make a well in the center and pour in the egg-apricot mixture. Stir until the dry ingredients are just moistened. Fold in the grated zucchini.

Line microwavable cupcake pans with paper liners. Half fill each with the batter.

Combine the remaining 3 tablespoons of flour with

the rolled oats, the remaining brown sugar, the walnuts and the remaining ¼ teaspoon of cinnamon. Cut in the butter until the mixture is crumbly. Top each muffin with 1 tablespoon of the crumb mixture. Microwave 6 muffins at a time on Medium (50 percent) for 4 minutes, rotating the pan a half turn after 2 minutes. Remove the muffins from the pans.

Repeat the cooking procedure with the remaining batter. Serve the muffins warm.

Apple-Pear Sauce

Serves 6 to 8

When you have softened the apple and pear slices in the microwave this is splendidly simple to make. Cut the slices as uniformly as possible for even cooking.

> 3 medium-size tart, firm apples, peeled, cored
> and sliced
> 2–3 ripe pears, peeled, cored and sliced
> ⅓ cup water
> ⅔ cup sugar
> 1 teaspoon cinnamon
> ½ teaspoon ground nutmeg

Put the sliced apples and pears and the water in a 2-quart microwavable casserole and cover with transparent wrap. Microwave on High (100 percent) for 8 to 10 minutes until the fruit is fork-tender. Stir once after 4 to 5 minutes.

Add the sugar, cinnamon and nutmeg. Mash with a fork until thoroughly blended. For a very smooth texture, process to a puree in a blender or food processor.

Spoon this fruit puree into bowls and serve it instead of applesauce with gingersnaps or by itself.

Caramel Corn

Makes 5 quarts

Melt squares of caramel candies in the microwave combined with a little water. Spread the mixture out on buttered wax paper and roll apples in it to make toffee apples—a sweet snack everyone loves.

This candied popcorn is fun to make—and so easy that the kids can help cook it as well as eat it. Use a medium-sized plain brown bag from the supermarket and make sure to give it a really good shake every 45 seconds. Pop the corn first in the microwave, using any of the unflavored brands on the market.

> *1 cup packed brown sugar*
> *8 tablespoons (4 ounces) butter*
> *¼ cup corn syrup*
> *½ teaspoon salt*
> *½ teaspoon baking soda*
> *5 quarts popped popcorn*

Put the brown sugar, butter, corn syrup and salt in a 2-quart glass measure. Microwave on High (100 percent) for 2 minutes until the butter melts. Stir and microwave on High (100 percent) for 1½ minutes more. Take the measure from the microwave and stir in the baking soda.

Spray the inside of the brown paper bag with vegetable cooking spray. Put the popcorn in the bag and pour the syrup over the popcorn. Fold over the top of the bag. Microwave on High (100 percent) for 45 seconds. Remove the bag from the microwave and shake well. Repeat the procedure 2 more times for a total of 2¼ minutes.

Spread the caramel corn on wax paper to cool.

Peanut Almond Brittle

Makes 1 pound

Who doesn't love peanut brittle? And when almonds are included, it is even better. With a microwave, the candy is easy to make.

> *1 cup sugar*
> *½ cup light corn syrup*
> *1 cup unsalted, unroasted peanuts*
> *½ cup whole unblanched almonds*
> *1 tablespoon (½ ounce) butter*
> *1½ teaspoons vanilla extract*
> *⅛ teaspoon salt*
> *1½ teaspoons baking soda*

Combine the sugar, corn syrup, peanuts and almonds in a 1-quart glass measure. Microwave on High (100 percent) for 7 minutes, stirring well after 4 minutes, until the sugar dissolves and the syrup is hot.

Add the butter, vanilla and salt and stir well. Microwave on High (100 percent) for 3½ to 4 minutes or until golden brown. Add the baking soda and stir to blend. Pour the mixture into a lightly oiled jelly-roll pan and allow it to cool. When the brittle is cool, break it into pieces.

Fruity Granola

Makes about 7 cups

A good snack to have on hand for after-school hand-outs, long car trips, movies and TV viewing.

> *3 cups quick-cooking rolled oats*
> *1 cup shredded coconut*
> *1 cup sliced almonds*
> *½ cup packed brown sugar*
> *4 tablespoons (2 ounces) butter, melted*
> *1 teaspoon vanilla extract*
> *1½ teaspoons cinnamon*
> *½ teaspoon salt*
> *⅔ cup raisins*
> *1 cup chopped dates*

Combine the oats, coconut and almonds in a bowl. Blend together the brown sugar, butter, vanilla, cinnamon and salt in another bowl. Combine the mixtures and stir well.

Spread the mixture in an 11-by-7-by-2-inch microwavable dish. Microwave on High (100 percent) for 8 minutes, stirring every 2 minutes. Rotate the dish a half turn after 4 minutes. Remove from the microwave.

Stir in the raisins and dates. Cool the granola and then store it in a container with a tight-fitting lid.

Blanch almonds by microwaving 1 cup of water until boiling. Add the nuts and microwave on High (100 percent) for about 30 seconds. The skins will slip off easily.

INDEX